A Child's Book
❖ of Prayers ❖

A Child's Book
✤ of Prayers ✤

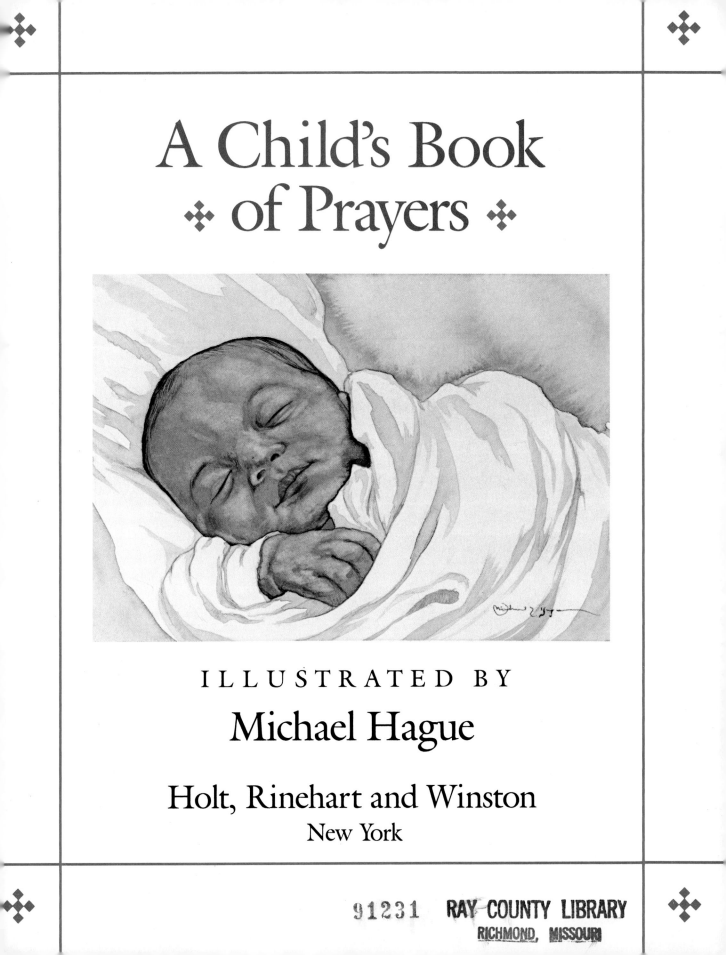

ILLUSTRATED BY
Michael Hague

Holt, Rinehart and Winston
New York

This book is dedicated to Geneva Pearl Inman.

Illustrations copyright © 1985 by Oak, Ash and Thorn, Ltd.
All rights reserved, including the right to reproduce this
book or portions thereof in any form.
Published by Holt, Rinehart and Winston,
383 Madison Avenue, New York, New York 10017.
Published simultaneously in Canada by Holt, Rinehart and
Winston of Canada, Limited.

Library of Congress Cataloging in Publication Data
Main entry under title:

A Child's book of prayers.

Summary: A collection of short prayers and devotions,
including both traditional or anonymous pieces and works
by such authors as Christina Rossetti and Robert Browning.
1. Children—Prayer-books and devotions—English.
[1. Prayer books and devotions]   I. Hague, Michael, ill.
BV4870.C44   1985   242'.82   85-8380
ISBN: 0-03-001412-3

First Edition
Printed in the United States of America
1 3 5 7 9 10 8 6 4 2

Offset Printing and Binding: Krueger, New Berlin, Wisconsin
Color Separations: Offset Separations Corporation, Turin, Italy
Composition: Waldman Graphics, Inc., Pennsauken, New Jersey

Designer: Marc Cheshire
Production Editors: Trent Duffy and Victoria Mathews
Production Manager: Karen Gillis

ISBN 0-03-001412-3

LET the words of my mouth,
and the meditation of my heart,
be acceptable in Thy sight, O Lord,
my strength, and my redeemer.

Psalm 19

Lᴏʀᴅ, teach me all that I should know;
In grace and wisdom I may grow;
The more I learn to do Thy will,
The better may I love Thee still.

Isaac Watts

DEAR Father, hear and bless
Thy beasts and singing birds,
And guard with tenderness
Small things that have no words.

Anonymous

ALL things bright and beautiful,
    All creatures, great and small,
All things wise and wonderful,
    The Lord God made them all.

Each little flower that opens,
    Each little bird that sings,
He made their glowing colors,
    He made their tiny wings.

The tall trees in the greenwood,
    The meadows where we play,
The rushes by the water
    We gather every day—

He gave us eyes to see them,
    And lips that we might tell
How great is God Almighty,
    Who has made all things well.

Cecil Francis Alexander

O God, make us children of quietness and heirs of peace.
Amen.

St. Clement

FOR what we are about to receive
May the Lord make us truly thankful.
Amen.

Anonymous

W<small>HAT</small> can I give Him,
    Poor as I am?
If I were a shepherd,
    I would bring Him a lamb.

If I were a wise man,
    I would do my part—
Yet what can I give Him,
    Give my heart.

Christina Rossetti

MATTHEW, Mark, Luke, and John,
Bless the bed that I lie on.
Four corners to my bed,
Four angels round my head,
One to watch and one to pray
And two to bear my soul away.

Traditional

O God, I thank Thee for all
the joy I have had in life.

Earl Brithnoth

I see the moon,
    And the moon sees me;
God bless the moon,
    And God bless me.

Anonymous

THE lark's on the wing;
The snail's on the thorn:
God's in His Heaven—
All's right with the world!

Robert Browning

GOD made the world so broad and grand,
Filled with blessings from His hand.

He made the sky so high and blue,
And all the little children too.

Anonymous

PEACE be to this house
And to all who dwell in it.
Peace be to them that enter
And to them that depart.

Anonymous

THOU art great
And Thou art good,
And we thank Thee
For this food.

Traditional

I pray that ordinary bread,
Was just as nice as cake;
I pray that I could fall asleep,
As easy as I wake.

Anonymous

D<small>EAR</small> God, be good to me,
The sea is so wide and my boat is so small.

Prayer of the Breton Fishermen

GOD bless this house from thatch to floor,
The twelve apostles guard the door;
Four angels to my bed;
Gabriel stands at the head,
John and Peter at the feet,
All to watch me while I sleep.

Traditional

DAY by day, dear Lord, of Thee
Three things I pray:
To see Thee more clearly,
To love Thee more dearly,
To follow Thee more nearly,
Day by day.

St. Richard of Chichester

The Lord's Prayer

Our Father, who art in heaven,
Hallowed be Thy name.
Thy kingdom come,
Thy will be done,
On earth as it is in heaven.
Give us this day our daily bread,
And forgive us our trespasses,
As we forgive those who trespass against us.
And lead us not into temptation
But deliver us from evil,
For thine is the kingdom,
And the power, and the glory,
Forever and ever.
   Amen.

Now I lay me down to sleep,
I pray Thee, Lord, Thy child to keep:
Thy love guard me through the night
And wake me with the morning light.

Traditional

Index of First Lines

O God, I thank Thee for all, 11
O God, make us children of quietness, 6
Our Father, who art in heaven, 25

Peace be to this house, 18

Thou art great, 19

What can I give Him, 8–9